PREPPER

How to Prepare for Recession and Inflation During the Coming Financial Crisis

(Long-term Survival and Self-sufficient Living)

Lena Hess

Published by Harry Barnes

Lena Hess

All Rights Reserved

Prepper: How to Prepare for Recession and Inflation During the Coming Financial Crisis (Long-term Survival and Self-sufficient Living)

ISBN 978-1-77485-107-4

All rights reserved. No part of this guide may be reproduced in any form without permission in writing from the publisher except in the case of brief quotations embodied in critical articles or reviews.

Legal & Disclaimer

The information contained in this book is not designed to replace or take the place of any form of medicine or professional medical advice. The information in this book has been provided for educational and entertainment purposes only.

The information contained in this book has been compiled from sources deemed reliable, and it is accurate to the best of the Author's knowledge; however, the Author cannot guarantee its accuracy and validity and cannot be held liable for any errors or omissions. Changes are periodically made to this book. You must consult your doctor or get professional medical advice before using any of the suggested remedies, techniques, or information in this book.

Upon using the information contained in this book, you agree to hold harmless the Author from and against any damages, costs, and expenses, including any legal fees potentially resulting from the application of any of the information provided by this guide. This disclaimer applies to any damages or injury caused by the use and application, whether directly or indirectly, of any advice or information presented, whether for breach of contract, tort, negligence, personal injury, criminal intent, or under any other cause of action.

You agree to accept all risks of using the information presented inside this book. You need to consult a professional medical practitioner in order to ensure you are both able and healthy enough to participate in this program.

Table of Contents

INTRODUCTION 1

CHAPTER 1: PLANNING 2

CHAPTER 2: FOOD LIST AND SAFETY IN FOOD STORAGE ... 6

CHAPTER 3: GET THE ADDITIONAL TRAINING NEEDED 13

CHAPTER 4: WHAT DO YOU NEED TO STORE 39

CHAPTER 5: PREPPING ON A BUDGET 43

CHAPTER 6: THE BUG OUT BAG 57

CHAPTER 7: THE BASICS 68

CHAPTER 8: MANUAL FOR BUGGING OUT AND CREATING THE PERFECT BUG OUT BAG 74

CHAPTER 9: STAYING VIGILANT 89

CHAPTER 10: FINANCES 94

CHAPTER 11: ESSENTIAL PREPPER'S FOOD LIST 113

CHAPTER 12: HOW TO BUILD A 'BUG-OUT-BAG' 122

CHAPTER 13: CREATE A SURVIVAL PLAN WITH YOUR COMMUNITY 131

CHAPTER 14: PREPARING BUG OUT BAGS FOR EACH MEMBER OF YOUR FAMILY 139

CHAPTER 15: WHAT SHOULD BE YOUR ACTION PLAN? .. 147

CHAPTER 16: BASIC FIRST AID 150

CONCLUSION 180

Introduction

The information in this book is intended to help you to construct the perfect bugout bag, one that won't disappoint you in a SHTF scenario. This book is great for those who have just started prepping and need more information on the items that should include in their bugout bag as well as those who have already taken on the prepper lifestyle and want to ensure that they're on the right path to prepping their bugout bag. Sometimes, the simplest of items slip us and we just need a bit of reminding of the essentials.

With the information in this book, the selection of a bag, the ideal weight of your bag, and so much more will be discussed.

We sincerely hope you enjoy reading this book and that the information within it is of great use to you.

Chapter 1: Planning

It is important you spend some time planning your approach to prepping for survival. Jumping in with both feet without a plan is going to leave you very unprepared. You will forget something along the way and it could be the very thing that jeopardizes your life.

When you first start thinking about what you need to survive, it is best to think small, short-term. No, you won't be staying in the mindset for long, but if you look at the monumental amount of work you have to do, you will get discouraged. Planning gives you the chance to take baby steps that are manageable. It will allow you the time to learn as much as you can about each element without glossing over any of the important details.

For the sake of this book, we are going to go through a process that has you planning for three months. This is a great starting point and allows you to slowly build from there. Once you get the hang of things, building up to 6 months and eventually a year of goods will be fairly easy.

Some elements that will need to be considered during your planning process are as follows;

Budget—what can you afford to spend every week/month on your survival supplies and needs

Space—how much space do you have in your home or a secondary location you will be retreating to

Where you live—if you live in tornado alley or somewhere your house is likely to be damaged, you need to consider storing the bulk of your supplies elsewhere

Climate—if you live somewhere the temperatures are extreme, you need to be prepared to deal with storage issues

Time—how much free time do you have to devote to the planning and actual process of preparing for survival

Family—you want the family on board, which means you may need to spend a little more time explaining and convincing them why you are doing what you are doing

Secondary location—this is a dream for most preppers, but the reality is very few can actually afford to have a second home in some remote area. If you don't have a second home, scouting out a place to retreat to is crucial, whether it be in the woods or a relative's home

Keep all these factors in mind as you go through the rest of the book. It will help you think about possible problems and how you can improvise to get around the hurdles presented.

Get yourself a pen and paper and take notes! In fact, get a notebook. We won't get into all the specifics in this book, but putting together a binder that will keep all of the goodies you find together in one place is ideal. The binder will keep your organized and be packed full of lists of what you need.

Chapter 2: Food List And Safety In Food Storage

Before going to the grocery store and piling up your cart with everything you'll find, it's important that we first go about the hows of food stocking. Here are the most important things to note in order to make your pantry prepping a stress-free experience.

You Don't Have to Do All at Once

You don't have to make a special trip to the grocery store and buy everything you need for your survival pantry all in one go. In fact, it's better to just gradually buy a little in excess every week to put aside in your pantry. That way, your goods will have varying expiration dates and you won't have to panic when they near their spoilage.

Consider Each Family Member's Preferences

While in catastrophic events beggars can't be choosers, you can still give your family better food choices by taking into account their personal tastes and preferences when choosing food products to stock up in your pantry. Letting family members eat food that they enjoy will help them keep their emotional spirits high despite the undesirable situation. Take closer note at special diets and food allergies, as well as the elderly, infant and pregnant in your family.

Consider Nutritional Content

While it is most important to choose food products that can be eaten without additional preparation like cooking or heating, taking into account their health benefits may be just as important. Choose food products that are high in nutritional and calorie content. Avoid those that are high in sodium as many emergency situations may also see you living on very limited supply of water.

How Much to Stock

The US Department of Homeland Security Federal Emergency Management Agency (FEMA) and the American Red Cross recommend that you maintain supplies in your home that will last your whole family at least two weeks long. If you are too worried about not stocking up enough, remember that when disaster strikes, chances are, you will also have sources of food from your refrigerator, garden, and/or kitchen cupboards.

Stocking on Shelves: Newest at the Back, Oldest in Front

When stocking the food products in your survival pantry, a useful tip is that you arrange your items by their expiration date. Place items with earlier expiration dates in front, and those with later dates at the back. This way, you can easily see which of your items are close to expiry, and you can easily consume them before they go to waste and replace them again.

Food List

Even though you will mostly be purchasing food items that will last long for your survival pantry, all of these products will still need to be replaced after a specific period of time, lest they lose their nutritional value.

The food list presented here is arranged by how long you can keep each item before it should be replaced, and is mostly taken from the list created by FEMA and the American Red Cross.

Consume within Six Months

Vacuum-packed meat

Dried fruit

Wheat Crackers

Granola Bars

Potatoes

Powdered milk sealed in boxes

Consume within a Year or Before the Indicated Expiry Date **(Many canned goods may actually last for two years!)**

Canned meat

Canned fruits and vegetables

Fruit and vegetable juices

Cereals

Instant oatmeal

Hard candy

Canned nuts

Multivitamins

Peanut butter

May Be Kept Indefinitely (Two Years or Even More)

Salt

Wheat

Vegetable oil

Baking powder

Sugar, salt and pepper

White rice

Dried corn

Dry pasta

Soybeans

Bouillon products

Powdered milk sealed in nitrogen-packed cans

Instant coffee, tea, and cocoa

Food Storage Safety

Of course, the shelf lives estimated in the food list are provided given that your food products are all stored and sealed properly. The safety in your food storage may be just as important as the food that you store. Here are important things to remember:

Store food products in cool, dark and dry places, away from direct sunlight, ranges and exhausts.

Keep food products away from petroleum-containing products like gasoline, paint, and solvent.

Buy food items packed in single serve amounts, or those packed in resealable containers, or transfer food items packed in plastic or paper boxes into airtight containers to keep them away from pests and rodents.

Dispose of canned goods that are swollen, dented, corroded or rusted.

Date all food items and replace them when needed.

Regularly clean your pantry.

Extra Note: Pet Food

When you have pets at home, remember that they should also not be neglected during disastrous situations. Stock up on pet food and special pet supplies, and replace them as needed.

Chapter 3: Get The Additional Training Needed

When you think about disaster preparedness, you may get focused on things like storing enough food and water for the family. However, that is only one aspect of the total package. In the aftermath of a natural disaster or even in daily living, you may find yourself in a situation that puts somebody's life in your hand. Car accidents, accidents at home or even shopping at the mall can turn into a deadly situation. It is important you learn how to do first aid and CPR. This can save the life of someone you love. In a disaster situation, it can take much longer for emergency responders to reach you. The 911 service may be down or overloaded. You have to be prepared to take care of an injured person's immediate needs in order to keep them alive until professional medical help can be reached.

Reading a book about how to do CPR or bandage a wound is not the same as actually performing the act. Hands on training from a certified trainer is your best bet. It doesn't hurt to have the whole family attend training. You never know, you may be the one who needs their help. The knowledge and training is priceless.

CERT

The government is well aware of what happens in the immediate aftermath of a devastating tornado, hurricane or earthquake. It can take hours or even days before first responders can organize and reach people who need their help. Sometimes roads are blocked and entry into suburbs and cities is completely blocked. We tend to rely on our ability to pick up the phone and call for help. We get to talk to somebody who can instruct us as to what we need to do until help arrives. It is almost unfathomable to imagine being completely alone with a bleeding person.

It is up to the people who live in the area that was hit to help each other out.

Community Emergency Response Teams or CERT is one way communities can come together to help each other out when disaster strikes. The programs are typically offered to groups of 15 to 20 people who live in one particular area. The training is usually about 16 hours or divided up into several classes. Participants are instructed on how to handle search and rescue missions, basic first aid, dealing with fire and HAZMAT situations and the psychological concerns that tend to follow a disaster. The more people who understand these things, the better prepared a community will be. You may not be able to call 911, but if you have a CERT team in your neighborhood, there is a glimmer of hope. Your group can give you that reassurance and help when it would otherwise be unavailable.

If you do not have a local CERT in your community, visit City Hall and ask about getting a program started. There may be government funding available. All it takes is one person to ask the question. If you live in an area that is prone to natural disasters, having one of these programs is especially important. Visit the FEMA site to learn more about the CERT programs currently available in your state. Talk with your neighbors and be ready to present City Hall with a list of names who are committed to joining the group.

American Red Cross

The American Red Cross offers CPR training and First Aid courses. You will need to check with your local chapter to find out when these courses are being offered. There is typically a nominal fee to participate in the class. A qualified instructor will provide hands-on training. Once you have completed the course, you will be given a card that is good for two years. Because techniques are always being improved upon, you will need to renew your card every two years by retaking the course.

In some areas, your Red Cross may offer Emergency Medical Response courses. These are more in depth courses that take several months to complete. Visit the Red Cross website, type in your zip code and discover what classes and training courses are offered in your area. There are some courses that are offered online. Remember, reading about. The Red Cross courses may not be offered, but you may be able to request an instructor do a class if you can show you have enough interest. The more people that sign up the less expensive the fee will be for each person.

Developing your family disaster supply kit

Let's talk about what it takes to put together a disaster supply kit. Each family's kit will look a little different. We don't all love peas and carrots or sardines. Experts will tell you it is a huge waste of time, money and energy to put together a fabulous food storage packed with foods your family has never eaten or simply doesn't like. Your taste buds are not going to change in the aftermath of a tornado or other natural disaster. Of course if things get downright desperate, you may be able to convince the pickiest little eaters to take a few bites, but who needs that kind of stress and frustration when things are plenty stressful as it is?

We are going to cover as many details as possible, but there may be some things specific to your family that are not included here, but you will need to think about. One way to cover all your bases is to take an inventory of what is in your pantry right now. Check the medicine cabinet and underneath the bathroom sink, too. Little things that you don't use every day, but know you have in case you need it are typically stored out of sight and out of mind—until you need them. Jot these items down or write them onto one of the checklists you have printed.

Water

Water is going to be your biggest challenge, plain and simple. It is big and bulky and takes up a lot of precious storage space. You can't do without it though. You absolutely have to have water in your disaster supply kit. You can live three weeks without food (but nobody wants to do that), but you can only live 3 days without water. You will start to get dehydrated within the first 24 hours of water being eliminated from your diet. Dehydration can be deadly when you are in a survival situation. It causes all kinds of problems and can interfere with the tasks you need to do to stay alive and to keep your family safe. If you didn't get how important water was, it is more important than anything else you could put in your supply kit.

Where a lot of people get confused about is the idea you have to store a hundred bottles of bottled water. If you have the room and the money to do that, you go right ahead. However, that is not always the best option for most. Consider this, each member of your family needs a gallon of water a day. Each of those little bottles of water is 20 ounces on average. You would need about 6 to 7 bottles of water per person, per day for drinking and minimal hygiene and food prep. A case of water holds 24 bottles on average. For a family of four, you would need to plan on a case of bottled water per day. Do you see where this is going?

You can opt to store the larger 5-gallon containers, which are still rather bulky, but at least you could assume you would use one of those per day for an average family. The cost savings is already fairly significant. It is also a little easier on your space. The bottles can be stored on a shelf or directly on the floor.

Now, if you have an available water source i.e. well, lake, river or even a swimming pool out back, you could simply store water purification tablets or a filtering device. Ideally, a couple cases of bottled water and a larger supply of water that could be cleaned as needed is your best bet. It will free up some storage space and you won't have to worry about the bottles or jugs bursting open and spilling during a serious disaster.

The rule of thumb during and after a disaster is all water is unsafe to drink if it hasn't been bottled beforehand. ALL water, even if it comes out of your tap. During any disaster, sewage pipes may break, filtration systems go down and debris can enter the drinking water system. Use some kind of purification method before drinking. You could boil it if you have a camp stove or still have electricity. The second water reaches the boiling point, it is clean. You don't have to let it boil for 5 minutes. Once that first bubble appears, the bacteria and viruses in the water have been killed. Boiling it any longer is a waste of fuel and water will be lost due to evaporation.

You can store your own bottled water in old juice bottles and old water bottles, but do not use old milk jugs. The plastic will break down in a matter of months and will flood your storage area. You will read about adding a drop of bleach to the water before storing it to preserve. While can do this, many argue it is overkill due to tap water already being chlorinated. However, a little drop of bleach wouldn't hurt.

Food and comfort food

While food may not be needed technically, most of us humans like to eat. Hardcore survivalists can go days or even a couple of weeks without food, but most people would really rather not and if you don't have to, why would you? Try explaining to your 3-year-old that while he may really be hungry, he won't starve to death for another 20 days or so. You also have to factor in the sheer lack of energy that accompanies not eating for a day or two. You are going to have a full plate after a disaster and need every bit of strength to start picking up the pieces. Your mood is also going to be tested. Staying positive is important. That is a lot easier to do when you are not starving.

Stock foods that do not require a great deal of preparation to serve. Those freeze-dried foods you see on various survival websites and in your grocery store are really the ideal option. There are tons of different meals that can be made simply by adding a little water. We are talking a thick, chunky chili, cheesy scalloped potatoes topped with butter and even desserts. While they don't taste exactly like a fresh homemade meal, they are actually very good.

Imagine being able to sit down at your kitchen table (assuming you are in your home that hasn't been destroyed by a storm) and eating a healthy sized portion of spaghetti and meatballs. The kids will enjoy snacking on the dried fruits that can be eaten as they are or reconstituted to be more "real."

A nice supply of canned foods is also very helpful. Canned fruits, veggies, meats and various meals are much more affordable than the freeze-dried meals. However, you need to watch the sodium content in some of the items. More sodium means you need more water to stay hydrated and if water is in short supply that could be a problem.

For those who are creating a food storage to last more than just a few days, stock up on grains and beans. Oatmeal, rice and flour will store for years if stored properly. They are also extremely affordable. You can buy 5-gallon buckets of these items for typically under $20, depending on the time of year and availability.

Don't forget to stock those comfort foods that are true necessities. We all have our different comfort foods. You know each of your family members best and are probably buying Cheez-its for Ben and fruit snacks for John and so on. Keep a nice supply of those comfort foods on hand. They can go a long way to making things feel normal at a time when the world around you is in chaos. Children are especially prone to having routines that includes a favorite snack. If they are used to getting a few Saltines before nap or bed, you want to have those on hand to help bedtime go a bit easier.

First-aid and kit

There is a strong possibility somebody is going to suffer some kind of injury at some point during or after a catastrophic event. It may not be possible to run to the clinic or hospital to treat the injured person. In fact, it doesn't make sense to take a mildly injured person to the hospital or clinic that is going to be packed with more seriously injured people. If it is minor and can be treated at home, it would be wise to do so.

You need to have some basic first aid supplies on hand to take care of nearly any eventuality. While you can buy a ready-made first aid kit, they tend to be a bit more expensive than if you were to buy each item individually in bulk. Bulk does tend to be cheaper and when you are talking about medical supplies, you can really never have too much. You could be helping friends and neighbors. You don't want to have to skimp because supplies are extremely limited.

Here is a fairly basic.

Tackle box or tub

First Aid book

Band-Aids, medical tape, 4x4 pads, splints, cotton balls, Q-Tips, ace wrap, gauze, dental floss, sling

Neosporin, wound spray, rubbing alcohol, hydrogen peroxide, scissors, tweezers, steri-strips, tourniquet

Tylenol (adult & children) Motrin (adult & children), Ibuprofen (adult & children), aspirin

1 month supply of daily vitamins &prescription medicine

Cough syrup, cough drops, menthol inhaler, sinus medication

Bee sting kit, Benadryl (adult & children), anti-itch cream

Anti-diarrheal, anti-gas, stool softener, laxatives, insect repellant.

Automatic blood pressure cuff

Stethoscope

Thermometer

If you have anybody with special medical needs, including prescriptions, make sure you have extra on hand. You can purchase a small bag for a couple of dollars to store your first aid kit in. A handy rubber tote with a lid or a tackle box are also a good option. It is easy to grab in a hurry and your supplies will be kept dry.

Make sure you know how to use your kit. Hopefully you have already signed up for a class and will have some training. It is normal to get a little panicky and forget what you are supposed to do when the pressure is on. Keep a small first aid pamphlet or book with your kit for you to reference.

Tools and equipment

You can help make your life a little easier by having some key tools and pieces of equipment at the ready. The tools you need will depend on where you live and the type of disaster you are preparing to ride out.

If you live in an area prone to hurricanes, you will probably want to have a good supply of nails, screws and plywood for covering the windows. Don't forget to have a hammer and drill to hang the wood. In the hours before a hurricane hits, you will probably discover all the sheets of wood are gone from your local home improvement store shelves. Stay ahead of the game and have this stuff on hand.

If you use a woodstove for heat or have one for backup, make sure you have a chainsaw and ax to cut the wood you will need to burn if it is cold out. If you are preparing for a winter storm, you will absolutely need to have a backup heat source. You have to expect the power to go out. If you are fortunate to have a woodstove, keep a few dishes and a percolated coffee pot on hand so you can cook on your woodstove.

A camp stove with extra propane tanks will ensure you have a way to heat your meals. Flashlights, spare batteries and a crank radio are all necessary items as well. If you have the means, a portable generator can help you avoid any loss of food that is stored in your refrigerator and freezer. It will also give you light, which can make you feel more comfortable and secure.

Kitchen equipment like a manual can opener, grain grinder and a hand shredder should be stored somewhere in the home. Sometimes it is easy to forget these items when we don't have to use them on a daily basis, but when you take away electricity, you have to learn a whole new way of preparing meals.

Below is a basic list of tools and equipment to store in your disaster ready kit.

NOAA Weather Radio

Local/US maps and compass

N95 Mask

Mess kits & dish soap

Flashlights & batteries

Pocket knife/Multi knife

Wrench to turn off utilities

Extra cell phone – charged

Paracord

Fire starter

Whistle & signal flare

AM/FM radio & batteries

Camp stove & propane tanks

Dutch oven

Duct tape & plastic sheeting

Work gloves

Extra can opener

Ponchos

Hand axe & hand shovel

Tent

Sleeping bags/Blankets

Walkie talkies & batteries

Lantern

Spare batteries

Biodegradable trash bags

Hand sanitizer/Moist towelettes

Clothing and bedding

Although you already have drawers of clothing and hopefully a linen closet filled with clean bedding, it is important you do a quick inventory of the kind of clothing and bedding you have available. If you lose power or if you are forced to leave your home, your clothing is your first line of protection against the elements.

For winter weather, you want to have wool clothing. Wool sweaters and wool socks will keep you warm and dry. It is crucial you stay dry when it is cold out to avoid inviting hypothermia in. Hats and gloves are also good to keep on hand. Most of your heat escapes from your head. Keep your head and ears warm with a nice wool hat. Your fingers need to be protected from the cold to prevent frostbite.

For summer weather, cotton is the way to go. Cotton will absorb your sweat and stay damp. A damp cotton shirt will help keep your body cool when the temperatures are soaring. Because of cotton's tendency to stay damp, it should never be worn during the winter. Also, avoid stripping off your clothes during the summer. A long sleeve, lightweight silk or cotton shirt will keep you from becoming sunburned. Don't forget your hat to protect your head, neck, ears and face from being burned.

Rain gear like ponchos and boots is a good idea and can keep you dry when you have to go out to check on neighbors or grab firewood. Never risk getting wet and chilled. One of the main rules of survival is to maintain your core body temperature. Being wet and going out in weather that is even a fairly mild 50 degrees is never a good idea. Your body will begin cooling in a matter of minutes if it is wet, cold and windy out.

Sleeping bags are great if you have to leave your home in a hurry. They are easy to grab and provide everything you need for sleeping. Keep a good supply of blankets in the linen closet in case you have to ride out a winter storm without any heat. You will need the extra blankets. Again, wool is always your best option.

Keep a supply of bedding, including pillows in your basement or the area where you will be sheltering. This keeps you from having to raid the linen closet before getting to safety. It is also helpful to have at least one blanket in the trunk of your car, just in case you are on the road when disaster strikes.

Special Items

If there is anything particular to your family that you use today, you need to make sure you include it. If you have a baby in the home, make sure you have diapers, wipes, baby formula and clean bottles. If you have pets, don't forget to stock some food for them and factor in an extra gallon of water a day for them when calculating how much water you need.

Although it may not seem important in the moment, having your child's special blanket or stuffed animal can be a huge help. You may not think to grab it in the heat of the moment so if you can have a backup stored away with your other gear it will help. Of course it won't be the blanket or toy, but it can help.

It is easy to get caught up with the basics. The things you know your family needs to survive without giving a second thought to the things that provide a sense of safety and security. Don't forget about the little things. They truly do matter.

Store a few things away that will help pass the time. When you don't have electricity, life can get a little boring, especially for the kids. Have a few books put away along with some board games and a deck of cards. It will help keep the kids occupied and out of your hair while you take care of business. Don't forget a book for yourself. You don't want to pass the hours dwelling on all the things that are wrong. You need something to take your mind off the disaster that has just turned your life upside down.

Chapter 4: What Do You Need To Store

This is one of the most important questions all beginning preppers have. What do you store? Do you just need to store some canned food or do you really need to store everything? Everything is the right answer! You have to assume there will be no stores. That means nowhere to buy food, clothing, medical supplies or even weapons. What you have in your home when things go sideways is what you have to live on for days, weeks or even months following a disaster.

You also have to assume that all services like water, sewer, electricity and even trash pickup are going to be stopped. You can't go to the tap and fill up your glass with water. You can't flick on the light to see. You can't even flush the toilet. Your home is going to be nothing more than a shelter with four walls and a roof over your head. When you are injured, you can't run to the hospital. If someone is threatening you or your family, you can't call 911. There will be no phones and there will be no police. YOU ARE ON YOUR OWN!

Does that help clear up what you need to store? In a nutshell—everything! Everything that ensures your safety, your general well being and even your comfort needs to be stored in your home. Yes, comfort is important. Surviving is as much mental as it is physical. You need some of the creature comforts to help put you at ease. If you have children, this is especially important. You don't want them to be in a state of panic. You have to be able to give them some downtime as well as yourself. Having their favorite blanket and snack can help give them a semblance of normal, which is extremely crucial to everybody's state of mind.

How Much to Store

The next big question you have to answer is how much do you store? This may boggle the mind as you begin to grasp just why it is you are prepping. Relax, it doesn't have to be as overwhelming as it may seem. You can take baby steps to get yourself to an adequate emergency storage. It isn't a race. Slow and steady is the way to go.

The government recommends you keep at least a 3-day supply of food, water and medicines on hand. However, most preppers are not convinced three days worth of food and water is going to cut it. Look how long it took New Orleans to get aid after Katrina. And that was only one city that was affected. Imagine how long it will take to get food and aid if there is a major event that affects numerous cities.

Because you want to slowly build up your storage, you should start with a goal of building up a 30-day supply. This will ensure your family has everything it needs to survive for at least a month. If you are talking about a typical disaster, like a hurricane or earthquake, this is usually plenty of time for aid services to arrive.

However, building up to a 3-month supply should be your goal. Some preppers go so far as building up to a year's worth of food and water. This is definitely on the extreme side, but is certainly a nice cushion in the event of a major disaster or act of war. It is important to point out that the folks who have built up an emergency supply that will last a year or more have been working at it for a while. It doesn't make sense to try and buy enough supplies to last a year all in the same day. We will get more into the specifics of food and water storage in the following chapters.

Chapter 5: Prepping On A Budget

Many would-be preppers are scared off because they assume it is incredibly expensive. It can be, if you let it. But for the majority of us, you may be surprised at how little extra time or cash is necessary to get started. And prepping can be done over a period of time and continuously. You do not need to run out and buy thousands of dollars worth of equipment and supplies today. You can slowly build your stockpile. Establish a weekly budget and focus on the necessities first. Here are a few more ways to prep on a budget.

Homesteading – We talked about self-sustainability in an earlier chapter. The more you can learn to do for yourself, the less reliant you are on commercial avenues for your supplies. Eventually, this saves you money. You can grow, can, and dehydrate your own food supply. A rain water system will allow you to become less dependent on the public water supply. Alternative energy sources can save you money over time as you use less public utilities and in some cases, can sell your excess to the utility companies.

Couponing – I know what you are thinking. People are already going to think we are nuts for prepping, now you want us to start extreme couponing? Hey, it works. It can save you immensely when we are talking about storing a month's worth of food for your family. Please do not expect the immediate results you see on television, but it is rather easy to save around 35% through shopping the sales ad and combining those savings with coupons from your Sunday paper. That 35% can then be used for your stockpile.

Thrift Stores – Second-hand stores and garage sales can be a great place to pick up inexpensive blankets and camping gear.

Bartering – We discussed bartering during a disaster, but that doesn't mean you can't get started early. Bartering is big business in today's economy. You may have things around the house you no longer need or want, consider trading them for some of the more expensive prepping goods such as a generator.

Storage Auctions – There are no guarantees with buying storage lockers, but you can come across weapons, camping gear, and precious metals occasionally. This is not something you should attempt unless you can afford it. It's a lot like buying a lottery ticket. You are not going to hit every time. You also need to consider what you are going to do with all of the things you don't want.

Prepping with Pets

62% of U.S. households own a pet. As a pet owner, it is your responsibility to ensure their safety during emergency situation just as you would your family. For many us, our pets are considered part of the family anyway! The last thing I want to see is your pets alone on the streets struggling to survive as we saw after Hurricane Katrina. Imagine the pain that comes with having to drop your pets off at an emergency animal shelter, not knowing when or if you will see them again as we witnessed with so many during Super Storm Sandy. A little preparation goes a long way.

The ASPCA offers rescue alert window stickers free of charge. These stickers are similar to those you place on your children's bedroom windows in case of a fire. The stickers alert emergency personnel that there are pets in your home that may need assistance. You can pick up these stickers at many veterinary offices and pet stores, or you can get a pet safety pack for free from the ASPCA if you sign up for their email newsletter at http://www.aspca.org/about-us/free-aspca-stuff/free-pet-safety-pack.aspx.

As was mentioned in the Bug-Out Bag chapter, your pets need their own pack. Here is a quick list of items to include:

· First aid essentials (bandages, antibiotic cream, alcohol wipes, pain relief cream, tweezers)

· 3-7 days of food (canned or dry – If canned, make sure these are pop-tops or pack a can opener, dry food should be rotated every two months to ensure freshness)

· Litter and a litter tray for cats (a cheap aluminum roasting pans works perfectly)

· Disinfectant soap

· Plastic bags for clean-up

· Food dishes

- Collar and leash
- Bottled water or filtration system
- **Toys**
- A travel pack for storing and transporting supplies. Special backpacks are available for dogs, allowing them to carry their own supplies if necessary.

If bad weather threatens, pets should be brought indoors. Establish a safe room away from potential dangers such as breaking windows. Designate an emergency caregiver in the event you need to evacuate your home and cannot take your pet with you.

Evacuation Plan

Depending on the disaster, you may need to evacuate your home. This may be an advisement issued by the government, or you may determine it is best for your family to leave. Maybe your home became damaged during the event or perhaps your surroundings have become unsafe. Either way, this is something to prepare for.

Your first order of business is to know where your local shelters are located. Even in non-emergency times, your local government probably already has a plan in place. They can advise you where their predetermined shelter and emergency camps will likely be located.

You should also have a few evacuation locations identified, along with alternate routes. If you have watched the news during recent natural disasters, you have likely seen how quickly main roads can become a gridlocked nightmare. Do not use these. Take less-traveled routes. You may plan to go to an out-of-state relative's home or maybe you have a second home or vacation cabin. Have a few options at varying distances to go during an emergency evacuation.

Keep gas in the car. We do not always have advance notice of when a disaster will strike. When it happens, and if evacuation is necessary, a large percentage of those around you are going to hit the gas stations before leaving town. Bad move! Try to keep your gas tank at least half full at all times. This will get you out of dodge and hopefully to a less congested, better stocked gas supply.

Creative Storage

You need to have a plan for where you are going to store all of your supplies. Many of us are working with limited square footage. You need to be savvy and sometimes, creative.

Obviously, you want to start with plastic tubs. These are inexpensive and easily stacked. You can get a lot into each tub and these will easily slide into the back of a closet or under your bed.

Can organizers and wire shelves are cheap and great for expanding your pantry storage.

Your car is also a great place to store extra supplies, but you need to be aware of temperature extremes. This is not the place to store food or water. But, your trunk may be a great place for extra blankets and sleeping bags.

Communication

Emergency Alerts – The government issues emergency broadcasts through three main channels; Wireless Emergency Alerts (WEA), Emergency Alter System (EAS), and NOAA Weather Radio. These systems are in place to inform the public of natural and accidental disasters. You may receive notification through text messages, television, radio or sirens. Calls may come by telephone or emergency workers may go door-to-door, depending on the event. Check with your local and state government and wireless provider to see what avenues are available to you. You can also subscribe to a privately-funded alert system at http://www.alertsusa.com/index2.html.

NOAA weather radios are readily available and affordable. Choose a model with hand-crank or solar-power backup, just in case.

There is always the possibility that you will lose wireless service during a disaster. Storms can destroy or incapacitate towers.

During large-spread events, lines can get jammed from overuse. Walkie-talkies can come in handy for communicating with your family over short distances. You can also invest in a Citizens' Band (CB) Radio, which will allow you to communicate with others and receive emergency and weather alerts (channel 9).

Entertainment

If you are cooped up in the house for days on end with no power, no television and no distractions, your stress level is likely to escalate even further. Plan ahead for easy entertainment. Remember board games? A blackout is a great time for a game of Monopoly or cards by candlelight. Paperback books are also an easy, inexpensive way to keep your hands off of things for a while. If you have younger children, create a "busy kit" with travel games, coloring books, etc.

Physical Fitness

Physical fitness is not something often talked about in emergency preparedness, but it is necessary. If you need to walk a long distance or camp out in the wilderness for a time, your body needs to be in shape. It is your most important prepping tool! You need strength and stamina to survive a disaster.

Exercise is free. There are no valid excuses. You can find 15 minutes per day for walking, sit-ups, and pushups. These activities do not require any equipment, just your own body. In an emergency, you are going to need the stamina and strength. Don't think about it. Just do it.

Chapter 6: The Bug Out Bag

The Bug Out Bag (B.O.B.), also known as the Go-To Bag, is a survival pack meant to keep you alive for a minimum of three days. The purpose of a bug out bag is not for long term survival, but rather as an emergency bag when you need to evacuate quickly.

Whether it's an imminent natural disaster, a chemical spill, or a terrorist attack that threatens your home, you should be able to grab your bug out bag and get out fast to safer ground. While in most scenarios bugging in at your home is a safer plan than bugging out to places unknown, part of prepping is being prepared for every possibility. For that reason, you should begin your life as a prepper by putting together a bug out bag to prepare for a home evacuation if need be.

The concept of bug out bags are immensely popular in the survival community, but there's a lot more to it than simply grabbing a random bag and filing it up with survival equipment. The size of the bag, the material it is made of, what it's designed for, and the specific gear you put in it are all very important. Here is the process you should go through when selecting the best bug out bag for you:

Volume and Capacity. When looking for a bug out bag, the first thing to look for is the volume and capacity of the backpack. However, this is something where many preppers run into confusion, because even though some backpacks claim that they can hold the same capacity, not all of those backpacks can hold all of the same amount of gear due to the arrangements and design of their compartments.

Look for backpacks that have multiple large and small compartments where ALL of the compartments can be easily sealed by zipper, Velcro, sealed pockets, etc. This will ensure that your backpack can hold as much gear as possible without losing any of it as you travel.

As far as volume is concerned, if you want a backpack that is designed to get you through a day, look for a volume of 40 liters/2,500 cubic inches. For a backpack that is designed to get you through three days, which bug out bags are traditionally designed to do, look for a pack that is up to 50 to 60 liters/4,000 cubic inches. For a backpack that is designed to get you through a week, increase the capacity to 6,000 cubic inches/80 to 90 liters. If you're looking for a backpack that can hold enough gear to allow you to survive more than a week...you're probably not thinking about what your body can physically handle.

Frame. Once you have decided what capacity you want your bug out bag to have, you'll then have to decide what kind of frame you want your bug out bag to be on. The two kinds of frames for backpacks are those that have internal frames and external frames. Internal frame packs will have an aluminum frame located inside of the backpack. They are significantly more flexible than external frame backpacks since they reposition the weight of the pack from the shoulders to the hips.

Additionally, internal frame backpacks tend to be slightly lighter and smaller than external frame backpacks, so if you're looking for a pack that has 90 liters worth of capacity to hold enough gear and supplies to last you a week, an internal frame set up is probably not the best option for you. But then again, the vast majority of bug out bags are only designed to last you for three days, so in that regard, an internal frame backpack should be worth your serious consideration.

Larger, stronger and heavier than internal frame backpacks are external frames. As the name suggests, rather than having an aluminum frame placed inside of the pack, the frame supports the backpack from the outside. The advantage to having an external frame backpack is the ability to attach more gear and supplies to it. Backpackers commonly use external frame backpacks in order to attach heavy duty items like sleeping bags, tents, coats, and so on. Another advantage to external frame backpacks is the space put between your back and the actual pack, which will decrease sweating as you traverse terrain.

All in all, if you want a pack to last you for a week or more, the external frame backpack should be your choice. If you want a more traditional, 3-day bug out bag, go with the internal frame for its lighter weight.

Build Quality. Now that you have selected the capacity and frame of your backpack, the next thing to look for is the quality of the build. Your backpack should be designed to hold up well in adverse conditions and be water resistant, the zippers should work without impediment, and the straps should be thick and adjustable. If you're buying your backpack in person, you should be able to tell if the material is tough and durable just by feeling and handling it.

If you're going for a deal over eBay or Amazon, it will be slightly harder to tell if the pack is durable, but online reviews and item descriptions should give you the information you need. Besides, if you receive the backpack in the mail and it feels cheaply made, you can always ship it back. The best backpacks to look for are military grade packs such as an Alice Pack or Three Day Deployment Bags.

Color. Last but not least, you'll have to select a color. Contrary to popular belief, you should consider avoiding more camouflage or tactical type colors, since it labels you either as a law enforcement or military person. When the grid goes down, you want to blend in, not stand out. For that reason, seek out more neutral colors. Green, brown, grey, or even dark blue should work well by allowing you to hide if necessary without making you stand out when you are seen. Avoid bright colors like red, orange, yellow, or pink.

Survival Gear. With this information, you will be able to choose the right bug out bag for you. The next step is the fun part, filling it up! As a hint, you may want to buy all of the gear BEFORE buying your bug out bag so that you'll know the general size and type of backpack you need. When your bug out bag is filled up, its contents must be well organized with the most important items in the easy-to-grab areas.

The following is a recommended checklist of items to keep in your bug out bag. Don't follow this guide religiously, meaning you can remove or add items as you see fit for survival in your specific location, but it is meant to serve as a general guideline for what you need:

BUG-OUT CHECKLIST

Electronic Items: Assorted batteries, 2-3 flashlights, GPS, Radio (solar), Radio (CB)

First Aid: Antibiotics, Aspirin, Bandages (assorted sizes), Bandana, Cloth, Cough Drops, Gauze Pads, Gloves (plastic), Ibuprofen, Mirror, Needles and Thread, Tape, Space Blanket, Tweezers, Tylenol

Fire and Shelter: Bandana, Candles, Charred Cloth, Clothes (coat, gator, gloves, hat, jacket, pants, socks), Cord, Cotton Balls, Glow Sticks (avoid red), Magnesium Flint Striker, Matches, Poncho, Rope, Sleeping Bag, 1-2 Space Blankets, Tarp, Tent (optional), Wool Blanket

Food and Water: Bottled Water (2-4 bottles), Canteen, Fishing Equipment, Water Filter, MREs, Protein Bars, Water Purification Tablets, Salt, Spices, Sugar

Hygiene: Chap Stick, Comb, Hand Sanitizer, Mirror (compact), Toilet

Paper/Tissues, Toothbrush, Toothpaste, Soap Bars, Sunscreen

Weapons and Tools: 3 Knives (Swiss Army-style, folding knife, fixed-blade belt knife), Duct Tape, Handsaw, Hatchet, Machete, Multi-Tool, Shovel (folding)

Chapter 7: The Basics

It's very easy to get started out in the Prepping world and begin to get the things together that will enable you to survive through an extended disaster situation. Of course there are many more things to think about and consider than what I am going to mention in this chapter, but to begin with, the first thing I would tell any budding Prepper to do is to get some decent food, water, basic hygiene and medical supplies together.

Water

Let's talk about water to begin with. Most people don't realize just how much water they really use on a daily basis. After washing yourself, you dishes and your clothing, flushing the toilet multiple times, drinking, brushing your teeth and cooking with it, you will have used a lot more than you think. So, you should always keep a backup supply of water on standby.

This is good to have anyway, even if you're not preparing for a large scale disaster. There are always possibilities of your pipes freezing or a water pipe bursting near you and leaving you without water for a few days. If this happens, everyone in your area will be heading out to the shops and buying up all of the bottled water.

In a survival situation you will need 2 gallons of water a day for general use if you're careful with it. It's up to you exactly how much you store. You may have a river running through your back garden, in which case you don't have to worry so much about water storage for example. But as a rule I would store 60 gallons per person for every month that you're planning for.

You don't have to go out and buy huge amounts of bottled spring water, you just need to get some containers and fill them with tap water. You could use empty drink bottles for this and just stack them up or you can buy large specialist containers to make things easier. You will need to boil the tap water when it comes to drinking it if you have left it for a while however. Or you can filter it without using heat, which I will talk about in the next chapter.

Food

Next, food supplies. The very basic things I would tell you to get in order to get you started out are rice and beans. Get big bags of both and start creating a stockpile. Rice and beans may not sound like the most exciting thing ever, but it does sustain life. You can supplement this with some canned goods and some other items which I will go into in more detail in the next chapter.

Medicine and Sanitation

The basic medical supplies that you should have in your home at all times are antiseptic fluid and a range of dressings and bandages. You should also keep backup supplies of painkillers and any other medications you may specifically require.

You should also keep a fairly large stock of toilet roll. This is very commonly overlooked but it's essential. If you run out then you are going to have to start using rags or ripping up your clothes. Also you should have some spare toothpaste and soap for keeping up your personal hygiene.

Lighting

You should also keep a form of lighting. As a minimum I would say a wind up flashlight is a great item to have and it's always worth keeping some candles and some spare lighters with your supplies.

That about covers it for the basics, the food and water is the main thing you should start getting together as soon as possible. These things alone will give you a big advantage over everyone else considering most people won't be able to last more than a week when the water goes off.

Chapter 8: Manual For Bugging Out And Creating The Perfect Bug Out Bag

Making the Perfect Bug out Bag

In this segment, will go over what things you'll need to have keeping in mind the end goal to make the ideal bug out sack. Keep in mind, each individual from your gathering needs their own bug out sack. I stock the majority of my packs precisely the same, with the exception of the attire, which contains similar things just in the distinctive suitable sizes.

The main thing you have to choose is the sack itself. There are numerous incredible alternatives out there yet I for one utilize an Osprey Atmos 65 knapsack. This permits me the room I requirement for my things in addition to it doesn't include a great deal of additional payload weight.

With everything stuffed, including my tent, it weighs roughly 30lbs.

This weight doesn't represent any nourishment and water I might carry with me. You'll have to include a couple of more pounds for that. I propose doing a little research and seeing what sort of alternatives are essential for your necessities. I experienced a couple packs before at last settling on this one.

I made a few changes in accordance with my pack like taking out all the interior sacks and changing over to ultralight sacks to eliminate weight. I likewise utilize pressing blocks to arrange my things and cut down on the space they take up in my pack. These works ponders for remaining better sorted out and I recommend you investigate obtaining a few.

I have my apparatus set up and composed into various packs. I utilize a survival instruments sack, therapeutic pack, attire pack, toiletries sack, hardware sack, tent sack, dozing sack, and my cooking set. Having these things isolated and marked eliminates the time I have to discover what I require.

Before pressing, I likewise lay everything out and twofold check my rundown to ensure I haven't overlooked anything. Try not to avoid this progression! You would prefer not to be in a circumstance where something you need isn't accessible in light of the fact that you were excessively lethargic, making it impossible to twofold check your pack.

Here I'll separate each of the packs and what things I keep in every one. Keep in mind, everybody's circumstance is distinctive, so don't hesitate to include or subtract anything as you see fit. There is nobody bug out sack that will work for everybody. Consider your area, your financial plan, and your abilities while finishing what you'll add to your pack.

Water & Food

The last stride of any great bug out pack is having the correct measure of nourishment and water proportions. Water is fundamental and you need an absolute minimum of 1 liter for consistently you think you'll be out and about. I generally fail in favor of alert and bring a couple of additional liters more than I might suspect I'll require. I 'd preferably the additional weight than not having water when required.

With regards to nourishment you need to have no less than 3-4 days worth in your sack. I jump at the chance to keep protein bars and MREs as my principle bug out pack nourishment things. You can include whatever you'd like however these are what I for one back my packs with. I ordinarily convey 8 protein bars and 5 MREs in my pack. I discover this is useful for 4 days, or even 5 days on the off chance that I have to extend it one more day.

Sooner or later, you may be confronted with the troublesome choice of either irritating in at home or pestering out to an alternate area. On the off chance that you've arranged appropriately for each situation you're odds of accomplishment will be much higher. In this area, I'll go over my own procedure for pestering out.

For one thing, if at all conceivable you ought to have a goal arranged out with provisions as of now put away there in the event of a SHTF circumstance. On the off chance that the world starts to crumple around you, ensure you know various departure courses out of your city or town.

Not setting up a bug out area ahead of time means you haven't done what's necessary planning and could abandon you in a perilous position in case you're not ready to find a sheltered territory that can address your issues rapidly.

Area

In an immaculate circumstance, you and your family will all be as one, and ready to impart when debacle strikes. All the more regularly, that doesn't wind up being the situation. That is the reason it's imperative that everybody who is a piece of your gathering knows the meet area to meet at, as well as where the end area is, and where the bug out sacks are found. In case you're ready to bear the cost of it you may likewise need to put resources into little HAM hand radios to better speak with each other if at any time isolated.

Elective Routes

It's essential that you have no less than two unique courses mapped out with various meet indicate end route the end area. Your first course ought to be the best choice if streets are open and there hasn't been mass frenzy. You ought to in any case maintain a strategic distance from significant urban areas however you can go through littler towns.

The second course will detail not just how to achieve your end area dodging all significant urban communities, additionally all littler towns, particularly any that utilization passages or scaffolds and cross some key landscape like crevasses, mountains, or water. This can be an overwhelming course to arrange contingent upon your area, yet it's imperative to do it, regardless of the possibility that it takes a considerable measure of work to arrange.

Meet focuses are imperative. You expected to set a couple of these end route in the event that you ever get split up or need to turn to another area in light of the fact that a region was bargained. You ought to have the capacity to conform your course from each meet point so you can in any case achieve your last area.

I keep calendars and maps fixed in tubes in each vehicle my family claims, alongside a duplicate in every bug-out pack. These maps are unfathomably vital and are dealt with all things considered. I've likewise made it an indicate rehearse the course with everybody on different events. It's less demanding to learn by doing it, instead of by taking after a guide with no genuine casing of reference.

Supplies

I keep my bug out sacks around 30lbs each. Along these lines there ready to hold all that we may require amid our travel however sufficiently light where it won't ruin our advance excessively. I went over everything incorporated into my bug out pack amid the last segment.

Timing

Timing is a critical component to our odds of survival, which is regularly ignored. When you think the written work is on the divider and your region will be bargained, it's an ideal opportunity to take off to your bug out area. Holding up too long can prompt to you getting murdered, harmed, caught, or isolated from your friends and family. It's ideal to leave early and not be right than to leave past the point of no return. In case you're wrong you can simply chock your bug out mission as a dry run, and come back to your regular daily existence with somewhat more experience.

Observation and Intel

Investigate your environment. Get the hang of seeing themes and assembling knowledge. In the event that the time ever comes, having those abilities will prove to be useful while out and about. It will permit you to settle on better and quicker choices with regards to progressing on your course and keeping away from conceivable pitfalls end route.

Rehearsing these aptitudes will likewise permit you to show signs of improvement feeling of when a crisis circumstance might approach, giving you a truly necessary take begin off to your bug out area.

Uniformity

In case you're going with a gathering, having a consistency of prepares can be a key consider your proceeded with survival. You need everybody to have entry to a similar key arrangement of things you'll require keeping in mind the end goal to survive. In the event that everybody is prepared in their own specific manner, this can prompt to openings in specific regions that one individual may have neglected, prompting to confusion and other negative outcomes.

Transportation

What are your arranged methods of transport? In most bug out circumstances, you presumably won't get far in a ground vehicle like an auto or truck because of clog on the streets, obliterated or raised scaffolds, and different perils.

Cruisers are a superior alternative, yet won't function admirably in case you're going with family, particularly if there's no place to hold with your rigging or additional gas. You can attempt to change a bicycle by adding saddlebags to the side, and some other stockpiling highlights.

Vessels are a decent alternative on the off chance that you have one and plan on heading off to an area available by water. You have to ensure you have fuel and additional parts on the off chance that you separate on the water.

In the event that you possess a helicopter or plane, that would be an extraordinary alternative however not by any means viable for the vast majority.

A few people take their vehicles to the extent they could and afterward taking whatever remains of their way by foot. While it's the longest and most troublesome approach to travel it additionally takes into consideration a great deal of adaptability, and gives you the capacity to stay away from recognition when required.

A Brief Guide to Bugging In

In this area, will talk about what you have to do with a specific end goal to legitimately bug in amid a SHTF circumstance. This has favorable circumstances and hindrances to bothering out. Here I'll talk about the means you'll need to consider taking keeping in mind the end goal to get ready.

To start with, take stock of every one of your provisions both sustenance and something else. You have to know precisely what you have to legitimately assemble a rundown of things you have to stockpile a greater amount of, and things you're great on.

Next, you'll need to take stock of all your home guards. Your home will go about as a protected zone from the confusion outside. Along these lines, you have to ensure it is up to the undertaking before an emergency happens. Being at home gives you leverage in that you'll know every one of the qualities and shortcomings of your home alongside the encompassing territory.

Having a decent home security frameworks with cameras mounted outside will permit you to monitor what's happening outside your home without presenting you to an assault or location. I likewise recommend getting movement locators that will turn on open air floodlights, so you can light up any individuals attempting to stalk around your property.

Introduce deadbolts on each entryway. In the event that you can manage the cost of it get more grounded entryways that can withstand a frontal attack. Your entryways ought to be made of steel and free of any glass. You'll likewise need a peephole as an extra minor security measure.

I additionally propose having locking security grinds over every one of your windows that can be opened from within, on the off chance that you ever need to get away.

Outside your home, you need least arranging to abstain from giving interlopers any sort of cover. I likewise have prepares set up so I can cover my windows so no light can be seen from outside the windows.

You'll likewise need to have a few weapons put away securely in your living arrangement on the off chance that the need each emerges. I have a little arms stockpile of firearms, blades, and ammo if there should be an occurrence of a crisis. I likewise keep bear splash in every room so on the off chance that somebody gets in and finds me napping I can achieve that shower and attempt and visually impaired my assailant.

You'll additionally need to have an escape arrange set up. This leads into your bug out arrangement above. Continuously be set up for each circumstance. The less supposing you have to do and the more activity you can promptly be taking the better.

Chapter 9: Staying Vigilant

Humans may be reluctant to accept change, but eventually, we do. We settle into routines pretty easily and preppers will do so more quickly than the unprepared. This has its advantages and disadvantages. An obvious advantage is that settling into a routine means you are not running around like a beheaded chicken; you are relying on your stockpile and keeping busy. You have everything you need and are not worried about what you will eat or drink tomorrow, or next week, or next month. A disadvantage is that you might get lazy. This is more likely to happen if you are not in a city where the potential for break-ins is much higher, but even in the suburbs of a city, life might become relatively stable and you start to relax. The best preppers are always on their toes, their eyes are always open, and they are staying vigilant.

Vigilant does not mean aggressive. Good preppers are not out looking for trouble, but they are anticipating trouble coming to them. As a prepper, you are at a higher risk for being targeted by looters because you are the one with the supplies. The stores will be the first to get emptied, and then everyone else who has so much as a roll of toilet paper is a prime target. The highest priority right now will be defense. This means fortified doors, windows, and strong bolts like deadbolts. Many preppers also stock sandbags to push against their doors as an added measure. Outside windows are booby-trapped with barbed wire, nails in boards, and broken glass in the window sills. Basically, anything that can keep someone away from your house is important for preppers. Good preppers will also be aware that visible defense systems can also alert potential looters that you have something worth protecting, but if your defenses are strong, that won't matter because once they try to make a move on you, they find themselves with a nail through their foot or facing an unbreakable door.

In terms of psychology, a good prepper in this stage could accurately be described as "paranoid." If someone comes to the door at night, a prepper is unlikely to answer, at least without a gun and without checking through some kind of peephole to make sure the person on the other side isn't ready with the back of a shotgun for surprise face-smashing. A prepper is also unlikely to share his or her supplies with just anyone. Bartering is fine and dandy, but a good prepper is unlikely to share weapons with a stranger and is certainly not going to reveal where their supplies are and how many of something is in there. No matter how nice the person seems or how harmless, stage three is just as dangerous as stage one, just for different reasons. People have had more time to figure out where the supplies are and they are desperate. Morals and restraint tend to fall by the wayside when water and food are hard to get, and a family is waiting back home.

Good preppers have to harden their hearts at least a little for the sake of their own families' protection. Different people will compromise at different times; for example, if a woman with a newborn baby shows up at your doorstep and needs powdered milk, there are a few ways to go out about this. Some preppers just will not risk it and send her on her way. Others will relent and bring her the milk. The smartest prepper will help her, but arrange a meeting away from the house. The woman might have a gun and as soon as you turn around, rush into your house and threaten you, or she is being used as bait by a group. If you arrange to meet elsewhere, no one has the chance to see your supplies and you can come armed with a group just in case.

The best preppers will rely on trustworthy relationships for protection and bartering during this stage. This was part of the pre-SHTF chapter and becomes vital during stage 3. You can also stay hunkered down alone for a certain length of time; eventually, you will need help, either in terms of replenishing your stockpile or because you need medical attention. If you have not spent any time getting to know people around you or moving with a group to start a symbiotic commune, you will be hard-pressed to find someone you know you can trust. If you are faced with a situation where you have to seek help from strangers or someone you are not sure about, treat them as you would someone who comes to your door in the middle of the night: with great caution.

Chapter 10: Finances

Have a Financial Plan in Place

An important step that many preppers seem to forget about is their finances. If the electricity goes down, you wont be using your credit or debit cards so you need to have everything thought through before the SHTF.

Depending on the disaster at hand, banks may be closed and you might not have access to your money from the ATMs. It is uncertain if our national currency will even have much value following a collapse. Goods will no longer get delivered which means that their costs would skyrocket. It would not take long for any cash that you store to be eaten up. Without money, what can you do?

Well, the simple answer is that we will need to go back to creating value in the exchange of goods and services. A much more logical transaction would be a loaf of bread in exchange for some manual labor instead of flakes of gold for food.

For those in the US, ammunition is going to be the item to stock up on. It is easy to store and will have much more value than any gold or worthless cash. People will not only need to be able to protect themselves but they will need to be able to hunt in order to feed their families.

First off, I am not one of those guys that believe that gold is the way to go. Sure it is a precious metal right now but only because we believe it to be precious. Following a doomsday scenario, it could become worthless. It is hard to break down for smaller transactions and its value can fluctuate wildly.

The idea is to not think about cash right now but to consider stocking up on supplies that can then be used to exchange for anything that you and your family will need.

Surviving Job Loss

It is no surprise that the economy has taken a nose dive lately and with it, it has taken plenty of jobs. This situation will get worse before it gets better. If you are one of the victims and you have lost your job, it is time to get your finances in order.

Don't Bash the Boss

It becomes very easy to take your anger out on your boss but if you were good at what you did, he will become a valuable reference for your next job. Cause a scene and I guarantee you that it will not stay within those office walls. Others in the industry will hear about it including anybody that you hoped to get hired by. Remain professional at all times.

Tally Up

Following a job loss it is very important that you take the time to tally up your monthly expenses and create a budget.

Depending on how good you have been at saving or if you have got investments, you may have more time than you first realized to find another job.

Government Benefits

If you have just come out of a job, this can be a pretty embarrassing step but it is something that needs to be done straight away as it will take time to be processed.

Cut Back

The next step is to look at those luxuries that you just don't need. This may be extra cable channels that you don't even watch or your cell phone minutes.

Prioritize Bills

Bills should never be left unpaid but as money gets tight, you need to start prioritizing those bills and understanding which ones need to be paid off first.

Call your Creditors

This may seem like a fairly strange step but in many cases, creditors may be willing to offer you a minimum payment that they will accept. Tell them upfront and they are much more likely to be reasonable.

Other than the tips laid out above, you need to remain positive at all times. It is not the end of the world just because you lost your job and I am sure it would not take too long before you found yourself back in work.

Getting Out of Debt

Getting control of your financial mess can seem incredibly difficult but with a few simple changes, you can learn to better manage your money and get your finances back under control.

Working it Out

The first step is to actually work out everything that you owe and who you owe it to. You MUST be honest with yourself otherwise you will only be creating more problems for yourself in the future.

If your debt repayments take more than 20 per cent of your net monthly income you are entering a danger zone and must take steps to cut back.

Budgeting

Once you have worked out and taken note of what you actually owe, it is time to draw up a budget. This will include a schedule for repaying your debts. It is important that you remain realistic and work out what you can afford to repay whilst staying within your budget.

Discipline

It can become all too easy to borrow more money to pay off existing debts but you must remain disciplined and not borrow anything more until your debts have been repaid.

Take Note of Your Spending

If you find yourself constantly getting in to debt, you should consider taking out a set amount of money from your bank account at the start of the week and then giving your bank card to a family member or friend for safe-keeping. By doing this, you can not spend more than what you have in cash.

Organize

You should make sure that all utility bills are paid via direct debit. This makes it much easier to pay off because you wont need to worry about sending checks on time. Most providers also offer discounts when you are paying via direct debit.

Switch Energy Suppliers

Before setting up your direct debits, consider switching suppliers as this could save you hundreds a year on your gas, electricity, water, and phone bills.

Get Rid of the Store Cards

When it comes to the highest rates for credit, store cards come out on top. If these debts are the ones that you are finding hard to manage, cut up and throw out your cards to avoid temptation. It is always better to pay cash for goods. If you cant pay cash, then shop around for the best deals.

Get Your Bank Account in Order

If you are customer of any one of the high street banks then there is a good chance that you are not getting the best deal on your overdrafts or interest rates. You could save a lot of money by simply switching to a current account and in most cases UK banks will pay you to transfer all your accounts over to them.

Switch Your Mortgage

A mortgage usually takes the biggest chunk of cash every month which means that it is very important to make sure that you are getting the best deal. Speak to an independent financial adviser or a broker about your re-mortgaging options and if it looks like you could save money make the switch. Remember to take into account any transfer charges from your current provider and any legal fees for switching.

Stashing Your Cash

It is always a good idea to have cash hidden away for emergencies. By this, I do not mean that you should go and hide it under your mattress. Burglars would not have a very hard time finding your cash if you choose to hide it there. So where can you stash your cash?

Envelopes

Just hiding your cash in envelopes would obviously be very easy to be found but the idea is to be a little creative here. If you have low shelving in the kitchen, you could tape the envelope to the underside of the shelf. Have a cat? Tape it to the bottom of the litter tray (underneath). Or how about taping the envelope to the back of a picture or wall decoration?

Toilet Flush Tank

You know that tank at the back of the toilet? That makes a great stash place for your money and valuables. All you need is a watertight container and you are done.

Sock Drawer

Here is a tip to put all those mysterious odd socks to use. They always manage to lose their other half but how about you place your money in to these and stash them in the bottom of your sock drawer?

Shirt Pocket

Pick a random shirt that is hanging up in the closet and the pocket of that shirt will become your stash place.

Bookshelf

If you have plenty of books on the bookshelf, pick one or two at random and stash your money between the pages or better yet, hollow it out and stash your cash inside.

Bury It

No burglar would ever break in to your house and then head outside to dig up your yard. Consider placing your money in a glass jar and then burying it in the yard.

Inside the Flour

Place your money inside a little baggie and then place it in the middle of the flour container. You could also do this with the sugar or coffee container.

Tampon Box

I am pretty sure your cash will be safe if you hide it in a tampon box.

Dirty Laundry

I don't think there will be many criminals out there that will stick around long enough to go through your dirty laundry hamper.

Inside Your Doors

If you have solid wooden doors, you can chisel out a niche in the top of the door.

You can run this 2-3 inches deep and can be a very good hiding place for more than just cash.

Inside Curtain Rods

Metal curtain rods are hollow and the ends can usually be removed. Pull the end off and you have a great ready-made stash place for your cash.

Making Money for Your Prepping

It doesn't matter if you gradually grow your supplies or go all in from the start. Prepping costs money. The best method for growing your food supply up is to instead of going to the store to buy a tin of tuna, buy two, one for now and one for storage. This goes for any food item that you choose to buy. For most of us money is tight so during this post we are going to cover a few ideas for how you can raise extra money for funding your prepping.

1. Work from Home

Starting a home based business in my opinion, is a great one which is why I have made it tip 1. This is nowhere near as hard as a lot of people seem to think it is. All you need to think about is what you enjoy doing and then how you can make money from it. Do you like teaching? Offer online tutoring. Do you like building stuff? Build it and advertise it for sale on an online store. Like to write? write a book. You get the idea. Think of a hobby then think of how to earn from it.

2. eBay

Another method that can make a nice side income is eBay. Like I mentioned above, you can build something and sell it on eBay or just have a walk around your house or go up in to the loft and find items you no longer need but that others might. By simply searching on eBay for those same items and you will see the kind of prices that those items are fetching.

3. Offer your Skills

Somebody always needs something doing but do not want to pay the stupidly high charges that many big companies are charging. No matter what your skills are, place advertisements and wait for the phone to ring. It doesn't matter whether it is painting, gardening, welding, etc. It will always be needed by somebody.

4. Yard/Garage Sale

Just like selling your stuff on eBay but offline, try having a yard sale or a garage sale for selling your items. There are very few laws and in most cases you do not have to get permission from your local authority unless you hold more than 10 yard sales per year. Do bare in mind however, that it should be on YOUR property. Do not place anything on the pavements as it would then be classed as street trading which does have its laws.

5. Cash In

This tip is not for one thing in particular but it could be a variety of things like:

Send in your broken phones for cash

Send in scrap gold for cash

Send in your old CD's and DVD's for cash

Cash in your old printer cartridges to places like "cash for cartridges" or "Infotone"

If you have any scrap metal laying around, go cash it in for a little extra money

Visit the pawn shop and cash in anything you no longer need

Sell your old books to Amazon Trade-in

6. Sell your Story

Journalists are always on the lookout for new dramatic stories. If you have something you feel they might like send them an email. Different magazines offer different prices for both stories, and photos so check around for your best prices.

7. Rent out your Driveway

If you have extra space on your driveway, consider renting it out to others. Many people drive quite a long way to work every day so it will be better for them to know they will have a parking space instead of having to drive around in circles trying to find one. This will definitely work well if you live in an area where parking is expensive.

8. Rent out a Room

If you're renting a room out, you've two options to legitimately reduce tax. The "Rent a room scheme" and deducting expenses. If you don't want a full-time lodger consider setting up over-nighters for travelers and undercut the local hotels in your area.

9. Rent out Your Home for Films

TV production companies are always on the lookout for new places to shoot. There are quite a few online agencies where you can list your home for free and they will take a commission only if your house is chosen. How much you can make varies from company to company however, you can usually make up to £500 per day in the UK.

10. Get a Grant

There are literally loads of grants available for many things including doing up your home and education. There are grant search engines available that can help you find what you are entitled for.

11. Solve Problems and Get Paid

Business have problems that is you can help solve, you can get paid. If you feel like this is for you, then Innocentive is where you need to be. Again the money will vary however, I have seen some top problems in the past offering up to £600,000 for the right solution.

12. Help People Move

Moving companies are not cheap so if you have a large enough vehicle, offer your services to help them move and make a little extra cash whilst you're at it. Offer your services from a simple add in a local newspaper.

13. Fiverr

At Fiverr.com you can buy, sell, and pretty much anything else in exchange for a fiver. Please bare in mind however, that fiverr.com is in dollars so you get paid $5 but there are still some good earners on that site.

14. Pick Domain Names

Have a knack for finding good available domain names? Join PickyDomains.com and get paid. People advertise on the website when they are in search of domain names for their business and if you get chosen, you get paid. Again, these also pay in dollars but it is better paying.

15. Design and Sell T-Shirts Online

Have a knack for designing stuff. Try your hand at adding those designs or quotes to t-shirts and make a few extra quid. Look at sites like Cafepress.com and Spreadshirt.com who will give you an online store, create the designs and sell them online.

16. Buy Joblots and Resell

I know what you're thinking. You are supposed to be earning money for your prepping, not spending it. Well this one is kind of a win win situation. Whatever you have on your prepping list of supplies that you need, see if you can get it in a joblot. You can take what you need and sell the rest for profit. If you want a fire striker, let's say they are £1.99 each. Look on eBay for a joblot and you might be able to pick up 10 for £5 – £6 pounds. Keep a couple and sell the rest.

Chapter 11: Essential Prepper's Food List

The following list is one every prepper should follow when purchasing foods for their family to eat and to use as bartering items:

Water

Cooking oils

Beans

Rice

Oats

Pasta

Canned vegetables

Canned fruit

Canned meat

Canned liquids

Dried corn

Peanut butter

Flour

Coffee and tea

Honey

Seasonings

Nuts

Cocoa powder

Whey powder

Powdered milk

The most essential item any prepper needs, be it for a power outage that lasts a day to an ongoing societal shift, is water. We already know that a normal adult is supposed to be drinking 8 large glasses a day, and while most do not reach that goal, you are still going to want to prepare for a gallon of water per day per person when you're filling your storeroom. Large dogs need about half a gallon per day.

When storing your water, use containers specifically designed for that purpose, otherwise your water might begin to leak after some months. If you think you have enough water stored, store more. There are dozens of ways that we use water every day that we don't necessarily think about (brushing teeth, cooking, cleaning, bathing, etc).

Another important item to store is some kind of cooking oil like olive oil, coconut, and shortening. Some oils (like olive) don't last more than a year or two, so buy kinds that have a long shelf life. Coconut is especially good because it is packed with nutrients, is heat stable, lasts a long time, and can be used for a variety of other things, like as a face wash. Oil is a good bartering item because unless a person is thinking long term, they likely have not purchased oil for their storeroom.

Beans are a classic emergency food because they are full of important nutrients like protein, are easily stored, and last forever. They are also special because when you combine beans with rice, they create complete proteins, which are usually difficult to find in a single food item. The most nutritious type of bean is the soybean, which has just over 28 grams of protein in one serving. Most other kinds of beans – navy, pinto, white, kidney, and black – have about 15 grams.

Rice is another disaster food classic. It is pretty cheap and you get a lot of food from just one cup of dried rice. Jasmine rice is the cheapest, while brown rice is the healthiest, though it takes more time to cook and usually requires spices to taste like anything. Other rice types include wild, short grain, and basmati. You can also buy instant rice for a quick meal option.

Oats for oatmeal are low in saturated fat, high in fiber, and are great for breakfasts during a crisis. The only downside to this item is the amount of water it takes to make oats edible, but there are cooking tricks that use less water.

Pasta is another food that requires water to make it edible, but pasta dinners are very filling and are made of carbs that can replace the ones burned during hard workdays and stress from the emergency situation.

Until you are able to grow and hunt for food, you will pretty much be eating all your meat, vegetables, and fruit from a can. Stock up on a variety of canned goods from canned tuna and chicken, to corn and green beans, to peaches and pears. You can also buy and freeze hot dogs and sausages, but as soon as the power goes out, eat these meats first.

Canned liquid is also an important item as you will not be able to store bottled juice without it fermenting. Canned pineapple juice and liquids like apple last about 6-9 months, so plan accordingly. You can also buy canned coconut milk, sweetened condensed milk, canned meat stocks, and beer.

Dried corn comes in many forms, like masa, polenta, and popcorn. For making tortillas, finely-ground meal is the way to go, but if you just want a meal with little effort, corn grits only needs to be prepared with water and eaten with honey, salt, or gravy.

Peanut butter is a good food to cut hunger pangs and is packed with protein and fat. For the best kind of fat, make sure the peanut butter is organic. A couple of spoonfuls a day when you

are trying to cut down on food consumption can help replace lost calories and nutrients, and give you a boost of energy. You can also eat it with your oatmeal.

Flour is an essential item for preparing other foods, like bread, and is also necessary as a thickening agent. There are lots of flour types besides white, like potato flour, whole-wheat flour, and even coconut flour. If you or any of your family members have a gluten allergy, you will need to choose non-wheat flours.

The next few items will become very useful in bartering as well as for food. Coffee, tea, honey, and seasonings like salt, cinnamon, and sugar are usually considered "luxuries" (except for salt), and so will give you a lot of flexibility when it comes to making trades for other supplies. Coffee and tea are relatively inexpensive and easy to store, and will be in high demand when all anyone has to drink is just water.

You can also stock up on powdered drink mixes. Honey is an extremely versatile sweetener that can be used to treat wounds and sore throats. Seasonings and spices have been used in trade for thousands of years, and have many health benefits in addition to livening up pretty much any type of food. Salt is an absolute necessity so store lots of it.

You can currently buy nuts in bulk and their shelf life is essentially endless. Nuts are full of important vitamins like protein and fat, though be sure to get the unsalted kind so you don't make yourself parched from eating them while you raise your blood pressure. Almonds are especially good because they contain a lot of energy-giving nutrients.

Cocoa powder is another item that seems luxurious, but the best kind of chocolate is full of antioxidants and has a uniquely positive effect on everyone who consumes it. You can also store chocolate chips and dark chocolate bars to use in baking.

Currently, athletes and bodybuilders are the primary users of whey powder, but because of its extremely high protein content, it is an important item to have in a situation where protein-high foods will be scarce and conserved. You can mix the powder with dehydrated milk (our last item) to make a shake. Add vanilla or cocoa powder for flavoring.

Dehydrated or powdered milk is an excellent have for baking and putting in coffee. It even comes in goat-milk form. When mixed with water and cocoa powder, you can make hot chocolate. Look up recipes that use powdered milk and have them ready for when refrigerated milk by the gallon is a thing of the past.

Chapter 12: How To Build A 'Bug-Out-Bag'

A bug-out-bag is a portable kit, usually stored in a backpack such as a military style patrol pack, that contains all of the items needed to survive without assistance for up to 72 hours.

If disaster strikes and you literally have to escape with only what you can grab and carry at a moment's notice, having a bug-out-bag to hand could literally save your life.

There are many things to take into account when choosing a backpack to hold your survival essentials. Most importantly, it needs to be big enough to accommodate everything you need, so one school of thought is that you shouldn't buy the bag until you know what you need to put in it.

Another important consideration is that you will not be the only one heading out, so you don't want the bag to make you look conspicuous, which a military camouflaged bag or one with an assortment of survival gear strapped to it would. People will be desperate and if they can see that you are carrying a survival kit strapped to your back, they may be prepared to use violence to deprive you of it.

Choose a bag in muted colors and either buy a used bag with signs of wear, or use it yourself to get rid of the never used look. If you want to utilize the bags capabilities to hang and strap gear to the outside, get a rain cover so everything is hidden from view.

You may also want to consider having a tactical vest under your outer clothing so you still have the most necessary items if you get separated from your bag. An anglers or hunters vest is a good lightweight alternative to military and law enforcement style vests.

What you need to put in the bag will depend on where you live, your personal needs and the types of emergencies you need to be prepared for, so there isn't a one size fits all solution, but keep in mind that you may need to move quickly and packing more than survival essentials will add unnecessary weight and slow you down.

Here are some basic survival essentials that you should pack in your bug-out-bag:

WATER

Minimum 3 liters.

WATER PURIFICATION

Purification tablets or a filter bottle capable of removing bacteria, viruses, parasites and other pathogens.

FOOD FOR 3 DAYS.

Energy bars and field rations such as MRE - Meals Ready to Eat are convenient and contain all that your body needs.

FIRST AID KIT

For three days you should be OK with a cut down first aid kit.

Allergy medication

Antiseptic ointment

Bandages

Band-aids

Latex gloves

Painkillers

Prescription medication

Sterilizing pads

Wound care

CLOTHING

You may have to leave in a hurry and not have time to change into suitable clothes or footwear, so pack everything you need and change into more appropriate clothing and footwear when you're away from immediate danger.

A pair of sturdy boots

Bandana

Hat

Long pants

Shirts

Socks

Warm and weatherproof jacket

Warm underwear

BASIC SURVIVAL ITEMS

A tent or tarp and waterproof groundsheet for shelter.

Sleeping bag

Portable stove for boiling water for drinks and heating meals. Military style mini stoves or gel cookers are good if space is tight.

Small pot or metal cup for heating water and food.

A flashlight, preferably two so you have a backup and some spare batteries.

Matches and lighters, make sure you have both and carry spares. Waterproof matches are readily available and inexpensive.

Survival knife.

Means of cutting wood such as a survival pocket chainsaw.

Weapons, such as pepper spray or firearms for personal protection.

HOW TO PUT TOGETHER A SURVIVAL TIN

To be even a little prepared is better than not being prepared at all, so in case you can't even get to you bug-out-bag you should consider putting together a survival tin that you can have on your person at all times.

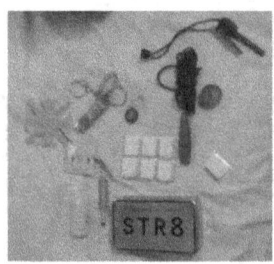

This really is the bare minimum of preparedness, but it could be the difference between life and death if things get extreme.

You need a small tin such as those used for boiled sweets or tobacco filled with the items you need to help you to survive in an emergency.

Here is a list of suggested items for your survival tin:

Alcohol swab

Aluminium foil

Antiseptic ointment

Band aids

Bandage

Dental floss

Duct tape

Emergency candle

Emergency phone numbers

Gum

Match striker

Military Can Opener

Mini compass

Paper clips

Pencil

Pin

Q-tips

Razor blade

Rubber bands

Safety pins

Small penknife

Small scissors

Thread

Tinder

Toothpick

Tweezers

Waterproof matches

Waterproof paper

Zip ties

Chapter 13: Create A Survival Plan With Your Community

Ask yourself a simple question: what is the best way to survive a disaster scenario? Is it to know how to evacuate a city to get to safer ground? Or maybe to know proper first aid techniques so you can quickly treat an injury before it gets worse? Or is to train in self-defense tactics so you'll be less vulnerable to looters and raiders?

Each of these things are undoubtedly important to know, but they're definitely not the most important things you need to know in order to survive a true grid down scenario.

In reality, the best way to survive a grid down scenario is to have an organized and effective team. Your chances of survival will always be significantly higher in a team then if you were to go it alone. This is because not only do you have strength in numbers in a group, but you can also assign roles to everybody so that each person is contributing to your survival efforts and so that you can assist one another as needed.

If you're still not convinced that being a part of a group is necessary for disaster survival, here are some additional reasons for why assembling a team will be to your benefit:

•You Make Friends Instead of Enemies

-Would you rather have your neighbors come to your door demanding food and supplies when disaster strikes, or would you rather work together with those neighbors to exchange resources and have roles be assigned?

•Strength in Numbers

-Again, strength in numbers will mean a lot in a disaster situation. You'll be less vulnerable to mobs or looters, you can more easily defend your territory and your possessions, and others will be less likely to even want to attack you in the first place.

- More Resources and Skill Sets

-The more people who are in your group, the more resources and skills are brought to the table. Each person will bring their own gear and equipment to the group, which you can then pool together, and each person will have a unique skill set as well. Within your group, you may have someone who is a doctor, a mechanic, a carpenter, a cook, a gardener, someone who was in the military and is knowledgeable about military tactics, and so on.

You get the idea. If you have enough people, it's possible to make a full fledged survival community rather than just a small team.

Regardless of how many people you have in your group, however, it's important that roles are assigned to each person to ensure that every member of the team is contributing to survival. These roles should be based on the particular skills or experience a person has.

For example, someone with a military or law enforcement background in your group should be in charge of training others in how to use weapons, scouting out the land to observe the best place to mount a defense, and patrolling the perimeter. A doctor would be in charge of gathering and maintaining medical supplies, tending to injuries sustained by members of the group, and seeing to it that your survival site is clean to avoid disease. A chef would need to ration food and prepare meals. A gardener would be in charge of growing and collecting crops.

Even the young and the elderly can contribute to survival as well. Children can be given simple tasks such as collecting water or lending aid to anyone who needs it. If any elderly people in your group are up for it, they can also conduct simple tasks such as mending clothing, washing dishes, and so on. Everyone who is physically able must be doing something if you want your team to be truly self-reliant.

Let's go over some tips you can use to determine how to assign roles in your team:

·Identify the Threats Your Group Faces

-Obviously necessary tasks such as preparing food or caring for the injured or sick will need to be assigned regardless of the disaster scenario. But before assigning other tasks, you will need to identify the biggest threats your group faces. Has the disaster happened because of a natural disaster such as a hurricane, a terrorist attack, angry mobs or looters, or a pandemic? You can only begin to assign roles and make a plan after you have clearly identified the biggest threat to survival.

- Assign Roles Based On What Your Biggest Threats Are

- Now you can assign tasks and roles to members of your team based on the threats you have identified. If the disaster has been the result of a large scale terrorist attack or if mobs and looters are in abundance, then security is of paramount importance and more people will need to be assigned to defending your group. But if the threat is pandemic or disease, then more people will need to be assigned to ensuring proper sanitation procedures and caring for the afflict.

- Change Roles as Necessary

- Don't think that once one person has been assigned a role they will be static in that role. As threats or priorities change, so will the roles in the group. In fact, some people may need to fulfill multiple roles, especially if your group is smaller.

- Hold Each Member of the Team Accountable

-If the consensus among your team is that someone isn't pulling their own weight, you need to hold a meeting to discuss this. The person you single out needs to be made clear how important it is that everyone contribute to survival, and that laziness or a poor work ethic is not an option. Each member of the team must be held accountable for their actions and how well they contribute.

·Set Daily Goals for the Group

-Your community should hold a meeting each day to determine the goals for the day. If your stockpile of food is running low, for instance, a goal for the day may be to go on a food run, forage for plants, or go hunting to bring in meat. As we mentioned earlier, roles in your group will change based on your priorities, including daily goals or an abrupt change in circumstances.

Your chances of survival will always increase when you're a part of a team or a community. What's important is that your team works well together, and the best way to do this is to assign each person a role based on their skills so that everyone is contributing. You can use the tips we have outlined to determine what those roles should be and to whom they should be assigned.

Chapter 14: Preparing Bug Out Bags For Each Member Of Your Family

It's imperative that you have a bug out bag on standby for when you'll need it. You need to have the items within the bag all packed up and to hand at the various places where you spend a lot of time.

A BOB that's at your home won't do you any good if you're at the office and can't get home before you need to leave the area in the event of a SHTF situation. So you need to have a BOB that you keep at your place of employment (or in your car) and one that you keep at home.

There should be a bag ready made for each person. Some people also like to keep a BOB permanently in their vehicle in the event that they're caught in a situation where they're not at home or the office and need to bug out right away.

Keeping a BOB in your vehicle is, to me, one of the better options. It is very unusual for me to be too far from my vehicle, at work or at home its always there so it makes sense that this is a good place to keep a fully packed bag that's ready at all times.

Your bug out bag must be suitable for the job ahead - to pack a bug out bag, some people use regular nylon bags like a bag that you would see used for a child's schoolbooks – not a good idea. You want to be careful with these. They're not roomy enough, they're not durable enough - and most of them don't have enough compartments to keep items separated for easy location.

Don't choose a duffel type bag that you'll have to hold onto as you leave. You want both of your hands to be free because you don't know what you're going to run into as you're leaving an area.

Other people choose to use larger, tough backpacks or military spec. rucksacks to hold the gear. Regardless of which type you choose to purchase, the bag needs to meet some basic criteria.

First, it has to be roomy enough to hold everything that you need it to hold to be able to survive for the crucial 72 hours that you'll be relying on the bag's contents.

The reason behind the 72 hrs figure is simple: You want to do one of two things – put as much distance between yourself and the SHTF situation, or you are making your way to your pre-determined Bug Out Location (BOL) where you will be safe.

Either way, it is assumed it could be a three day hike or 50 miles away maximum. Any more and you're getting into the realms of considering a Bug Out Vehicle as a means of escape.

If you BOL is further afield you plan must include leaving as early as possible before a SHTF situation really gets going. Uncontrolled rioting, a pandemic spreading your way, these are scenarios where you can pre-empt a disaster situation arising and act in advance. In these cases you may still be able to use public transport, although a BOV gives you a lot more options.

Second, the bag should be sturdy. If you spend the money on something cheap that's poorly made, you're betting your life on that material holding up. If it breaks down and rips from the pressure of the content, your items could fall out and leave you without if you don't notice the tear when it happens.

The bag that you buy should also be waterproof or at the very least water resistant. If you get a bag that absorbs water, it stands to reason that the content within will get soaked and won't be any good for use.

If you choose to get a backpack, you'll want one that fits your body type and size. With good support and padding to suit. It needs to accommodate all you supplies and equipment, yet not be too big and bulky. But most importantly, you need to be able to carry it and walk distances with it fully loaded.

In the event that you'll have to travel long distances, you'll appreciate this additional comfort. When you look through the various types of backpacks, you'll want to look for ones that say they're military grade or used for tactical manoeuvres.

These are backpacks that are like the ones used by the military and they're made to withstand a lot of wear and tear. These are also the bags that won't stand out. You want to make sure that you get a bag that is very neutral in colour.

If you're in a wooded area, you want your backpack to be difficult for others to see. A neon green or pink backpack could alert people that you don't want to know your whereabouts that you're in the area. So it makes sense to buy a camouflage or woodland patterned rucksack.

But, buying camo is a mistake as you are now looking like someone who's on a mission to escape, with a bag full of goodies. It's overkill, as is dressing up in full combat gear for your escape. Even if you were in the military, you do not want to stand out from the crowd.

Remember, not everyone fleeing from a SHTF situation will be someone that you can trust. Your best option by far is to choose a backpack that's made of darker, non-shinny material. A material that is a very neutral colour and doesn't scream 'look at me'...

A darker, neutral material will also blend into a wooded area reasonably well. If there's anything neon or bright on the bag, either take it off or cover it up.

Essentially you want to be 'the grey man' – seen but not seen. You need to blend seamlessly into everyone else and not attract attention to yourself.

BOB size is a vitally important consideration, and apart from the type and material considerations, there are only two points to consider:

1/ physical volume of the pack – can you get everything you need into it?

2/ physical weight of the pack – can you even carry it?

Part of your overall planning should be regular practice with you pack fully loaded and walking at least a few miles with it at speed. It is not as easy as it sounds! You may even need to run with it and I suggest this is tested out to see how you fair.

You do not want a bag that is too big and looks like you have the contents of your house in it. Again you'll stick out like a sore thumb and attract unwanted attention to yourself very quickly. Just a rucksack that is proportionally right for your body size and weight. That way it will all appear natural, you will walk naturally and comfortably with normal body language.

If you load a large, multi-coloured rucksack down with too much weight and you'll look like something from the ministry of silly walks.

Chapter 15: What Should Be Your Action Plan?

Most of us cannot make decisions on the moment and require some calculations to decide our next course of action. However in times of a disaster when your decisions could make the difference between life and death, you need to make decisions within a micro second. For starters the decision to stay put or get moving when a disaster strikes might be one of the most crucial decisions of all that needs to be made within seconds by analyzing the situation. You cannot take time to make your choice, it has to be quick.

You need to assess if your home is the safest place to stay depending on what disaster you face. For example if a flood is on the way and your house is near the ocean, you need to evacuate. However if you are faced with heavy snowfall and blizzards, if your house is constructed well enough to withstand the disaster, you should stay put. You must also listen to the official advice sent out by the government as they have experts evaluating the best of course of action.

If your house is made of glass, or is damaged in the disaster you would have to evacuate. You must also ask yourself how safe hour house is once the power goes out. Do not discuss your plans with anyone but your family as people might invade your house to loot your supplies. When the first warning sounds, cover your glass windows with plywood to make sure they do not break and hurt anyone and make the house unsafe to live.

Make sure you know all the routes around your house on foot so that when you need to evacuate, you know which path is the safest to take. Make sure your supplies are packed in individual bags and ready to go beforehand. Do not help strangers as they could be criminals looking for supplies from you.

Chapter 16: Basic First Aid

The vast majority of injuries outdoors are minor and easily treatable. When gathering resources in the wilderness, most of the time your purpose is to keep a circumstance from getting worse so you can continue on with your journey. That said, it is important to be prepared for any scenario.

The primary thing you need in a wilderness first aid training course is how to evaluate an affected person, which includes the following steps:

Evaluate the scene

Become aware of hazards

Take a good look: head-to-toe check, vital signs, and patient history

Make an injury and care plan, which involves an evacuation decision

Treat the affected person, providing each clinical and emotional help

Review how the patient is doing

We recommend you take a wilderness first aid class to learn each primary patient evaluation and ways to deal with a variety of medical situations. REI has partnered with NOLS Wilderness Medicine to offer that training at many REI stores.

Remember: protection is your duty. No article or video can replace the recommendation of either physician or professional instruction. Make sure you are practiced in the right techniques and safety necessities before you administer the first aid.

Wilderness First Aid Vs. "City" First Aid

If you have already had some modern first aid training, it is really worth noting that wilderness first aid may be different. There are four important factors:

Time: It is a long way to the doctor's office, and wilderness search and rescue employees can't respond as fast as 9-1-1 in the city. In the backcountry, it could be hours or days until your patient gets expert care so you want to be equipped to use emergency resources and to take care of that person for a long time period.

Surroundings: You can face extremes of weather and unique types of physical hazards than you will face in the city.

Resources: When you are administering aid in the wilderness, you are limited to what's in your bag and what you could use from your surroundings. Good wilderness medical training has to cover what to keep in your first aid kit.

Communication: Even with improved cellphone reliability, your ability to call for help from the wilderness is limited; that means your care might be the patient's only option.

Preparing to Give Wilderness First Aid

Say you are out hiking and come upon someone who is bleeding and unconscious. Your first instinct is likely to run to them to help. However, you want to make sure you do not become a casualty yourself, and that you know the situation before hurrying to begin treatment. That is why you want to follow these steps before doing anything:

Determine whether the area is safe: make sure no further danger is near—for both patient and responders. If a rockslide caused the damage, for instance, you would possibly want to move the patient out of the way of further rock fall.

Determine the Mechanism of Harm (MOI). Look around to determine what may have brought on the twist of fate or incident. That gives you clues to the type of injuries that are likely present.

Determine the number of patients. Do not assume that the most obviously injured individual is the only one in need of evaluation and care.

Wilderness first aid: initial patient assessment

After you have decided that it is safe, you can begin treating your patient. Your next steps need to be to discovering any immediate threats to the patient's life. Before you begin a preliminary life-risk exam, begin with these steps:

Attain consent to treat (if the person is awake). Ask the individual if you can help. If the answer is "yes," then ask their name, symptoms, and what happened.

Check foe responsiveness. Attempt to wake the patient if they aren't responding. (If there is a chance of a spine injury, you want to carefully place your palms on both sides of the person's head and keep the patient still.)

next, you will begin your life-risk exam. NOLS calls this "ABCDE" tests, using a mnemonic tool that will help you remember the steps:

Airway test: look in the mouth and take a look in the airway for obstructions.

Breathing test: look carefully at the chest; listen and feel for signs of breathing.

Circulatory test: check for a pulse and for wounds that are bleeding.

Disability test: If you can't rule out a spine injury, continue to protect it.

Discover injuries: without moving the patient, remove clothing covering serious injuries so that you can fully evaluate and treat them.

Whether you take a look at for predominant bleeding (C) first or for respiration troubles (A and B) first depends on your preliminary judgment on the scene. If you suspect a major wound, take a look at and stabilize it first.

Deal with any immediately life-threatening conditions found at any stage in the ABCDE exam. Those might include getting rid of airway obstructions, doing CPR, or making use of direct pressure to stop bleeding. As soon as the patient is out of immediate danger, you may start an extra-thorough exam.

Wilderness first aid: Secondary patient assessment

When you have executed your preliminary patient evaluation, you will accumulate statistics to make your treatment plan, make your evacuation choice, and to move on to medical specialists who later care for the patient. You may also decide to relocate the patient to a more stable, sheltered site at this time.

The techniques below highlight key parts of the secondary exam. A wilderness first aid course will take you through the technique detailed in each section:

First aid responder doing a head-to-toe exam of their patient

Do a head-to-toe examination: start by making sure your palms are clean, warm, and gloved. Then explain to the patient what you are doing: methodically going over all areas of the body seeking out clues about injuries or infection.

Your evaluation consists of several techniques for detection:

Look: for blood and other bodily fluids, discoloration or unusual shapes

Listen: for airway noises or uncommon sounds when joints are moved

Feel: for wounds, deformities and surprising hardness, softness or tenderness

Smell: for uncommon odors

Ask: if anything hurts or feels atypical or numb

First aid responder checking for patient's wrist pulse

Check vital signs and symptoms: record the time and write all of the essential symptoms down. One helpful tip is to write them down on a chunk of tape and place it on the patient's leg, so the data travels with them when extra help arrives.

Here's what you will take notes on:

Degree of responsiveness: Is the patient awake and alert? Wide awake and disoriented? Or is your patient subconscious or unresponsive?

Heart beat: using the wrist pulse, take a look at the wide variety of beats according to the minute and note whether or not the pulse is strong or weak; regular or irregular.

Respiration rate: test the patient's number of breaths by counting for a minute and note if the respiration is simple or labored.

Skin signs and symptoms: take a look at skin color, temperature, and moisture. The eye or lip are accurate places to check for color. Is it red or faded? Is the feeling of their skin warm and dry vs. cool and clammy? If possible, also record the patient's temperature with a thermometer.

First aid responder and patient discussing patient records

Do patient records: Ask questions to find information that will help you with your assessment and treatment. For instance, you could possibly find that your patient missed taking important medicines or did not drink enough water on a warm day.

To cover the critical topics, ask them about the following:

Primary complaint: What's your most extensive problem? When did it begin? What makes it worse or better? Where is it located? How bad is it?

What is their medical history?

Signs: Ask if the patient can offer additional information about the primary grievance, or if they have other situations or issues.

Allergic reactions: Are there severe ones? (Food and medications are common ones; also ask about bees.) What are the patient's reactions to their allergies?

Medicines: Get as many details as possible for both prescription and over-the-counter drugs.

Pertinent medical records: find if they have any clinical conditions that require them to see medical doctor for treatment.

Last fluid/food intake, last urine/bowel output: How long ago and what kind?

Situation: Ask if they know what caused the event and for information leading up to it.

Wilderness First Aid: Creating a Treatment Plan

Go over all the facts you have accumulated and made a treatment plan together with anticipated issues. Then comply with your plan while monitoring the patient's health closely and making sure that they are as comfortable as possible.

Taking wilderness first aid courses will help you learn about a ramification of medical troubles, and what you need to do for them, which include:

spine and head injuries

shock

wounds and infections, burns and blisters

bone and soft-tissue injuries

heat exhaustion and heat stroke

hypothermia and frostbite

altitude sickness

lightning-related injuries

Hypersensitive reactions (which include snakes, scorpions, and bugs)

Chest pain, shortness of breath, altered mental state

Making an evacuation decision: every time a situation is extreme, you have to determine whether or not to evacuate and by what approach: helicopter, carried by rescuers, or with you and the patient walking by your own accord. This is a complicated choice based on specific signs, how the patient is doing, the supply of rescue sources, and the remoteness of your location, among other things.

Wilderness first aid pointers

If feasible, have a person of the same gender carry out the top-to-toe examination.

Have someone help the examiner by using writing down observations and vital signs and symptoms.

Assign different tasks, such as boiling water for drinking or setting up place camp, so that the patient knows care is orderly and all rescuers have a role.

Try to keep the patient clean, warm, and calm. If you are waiting for assistance to arrive, things such as shelter, sustenance, and general nursing care might be key to keeping the patient well.

Fluids are more important than food; avoid caffeinated and sugary liquids.

Provide emotional support and empathy

Inform the patient about all aspects of care and involve them in evacuation choices.

Restock and/or supplement your first aid kit before every trip (do not remember a larger tube of antibiotic ointment and extra dressing materials, amongst other things).

10 Survival first aid suggestions for the outdoorsman

Venturing into the great outdoors is a favorite pastime for plenty of people. Each year, people spend their time hiking, rafting, and exploring the outside. But, there are dangers you should look out for a when having fun outdoors.

There is a variety of troubles you can run into, which include insect bites, infections, sunburn, snake bites, heat stroke, and dehydration.

Cold weather poses a whole additional set of demanding situations for campers, especially in those used to hot weather. People who have pre-existing medical conditions may also run out of medicine or have problems like hypersensitive reactions. While there are many situations to bear in mind, it is possible to have a great time in the wilderness and live safely. You just need to understand the fundamentals. Here are ten survivals first aid tips to keep in mind if you want to help.

1. Learn CPR

One of the most precious skills you can have in the wilderness is CPR. This stands for cardiopulmonary resuscitation, a method that uses a chain of rescue respiration and chest compression. The goal of this technique is to keep a person alive until help can arrive.

CPR is essential to preventing brain death. Rapid action can save a life. For CPR to be effective, the patient's body temperature has to be above ninety degrees Fahrenheit. Chest compression must be rapid and hard, on the lower part of the sternum.

The idea behind compression is to maintain blood circulating in the body, so it reaches the brain.

CCR

Another technique used in the discipline is CCR, which stands for cardio-cerebral resuscitation. This is just like CPR, but it involves only using chest compression, no rescue respiration.

Each strategy has the ability to save lives while in the wilderness. Before you leave on your next expedition, remember to take a CPR class given through the American Heart Association. This can ensure you have the right training to help those in need.

Know how to clean and treat a wound

Whenever you are in the wilderness, you have the possibility of being wounded. While as most wounds are not extreme and do not require a lot more than cleansing, others can be extreme.

An irrigation syringe is a critical tool for wounds. It may be used to run clean water over a wound once you wash it with clean soap. This facilitates disbursements of particles and contamination-causing materials.

Know what's in your first aid kit and what the whole thing is used for

A properly stocked first aid kit is an essential part of being outside. You could either buy a pre-made package or make one yourself.

Acetaminophen, ibuprofen, and antibiotic lotions are only some items you may want. Other essential items include sunscreen, a whistle, cellphone charger, and a water-resistant flashlight.

More information regarding first aid kits can be found at the American Red Cross.

Treat sprains

If you are often in the wilderness, you may end up with sprains sooner or later. This is a risk that plagues hikers and rock climbers but can happen to anybody.

Knees, ankles, and elbows are the most commonly sprained joints. Minor sprains are usually soothed using the RICE technique, which stands for relaxation, ice, compression, and raise. Use cold packs for the first 24 hours after injury. After that, heat packs can also lessen pain well.

You must have compression bandages for your first aid kit and OTC pain medications to ease the pain. Knowing the way to treat sprains before you are in the situation is key to getting the pain underneath control fast.

Recognize dehydration early

Dehydration can happen very rapidly when you are outside in the sun and heat, especially when you are moving. This condition can be sneaky, and symptoms can arise unexpectedly. Dehydration occurs when you lose more body fluids than you are taking in. When you are busy outside, it may be easy to forget to drink enough water or sports drinks. This means your body is in need of fluid, especially after urinating and sweating.

Dehydration can happen to all of us; however, toddlers and elderly people are at the greatest risk.

There are some early warning signs and symptoms that could suggest someone is dehydrated.

Those consist of not generating tears, dry mouth, skin that sags when you pinch it, and dry eyes.

When you have babies or small kids, it is always crucial to make sure they have adequate fluid consumption even when you are outdoors. The best way of treating dehydration is to prevent it from happening in the first place.

Dehydration may be serious. If you see the early warning signs and symptoms of dehydration, you should get medical attention fast to avoid extreme complications.

Treat burns efficiently

Burns are one of the most painful accidents you could have. Alas, burns frequently arise when camping in the wilderness.

If this happens to you, it is important to know the way to deal with burns successfully.

You will want to know the difference in treating chemical burns and burns from heat sources like the fire. Further, everyone in your party needs to know the way to stop, drop, and roll to prevent a fire from spreading.

The short motion reduces the amount of area burned at the body. Moderate burns are more easily dealt with in the wilderness than extreme burns. However, if anyone suffers a severe and painful burn, medical treatment must be sought.

Understand hypothermia

Hypothermia is the second main cause of death in the wilderness. When the temperature of the body drops underneath ninety-five degrees Fahrenheit, hypothermia can set in.

That is a life-threatening condition and requires emergency treatment as quickly as possible. Before heading out into the wilderness, you want to understand hypothermia and how to avoid it.

Hypothermia can occur when you are exposed to cold weather or wet conditions.

Being in cold water also can cause this condition to occur. Experts say that if you fall into cold water and can't get out in 5 to 15 minutes, you may not be able to get out without help. Depending on the temperature of the water, you have 90 to 180 minutes before suffering a cardiac arrest from hypothermia.

If you are prone to getting hypothermia outside, avoid ingesting alcohol. In addition to inflicting impaired judgment, alcohol dilates your blood vessels. This slows the blood from being distributed to the rest of your body, and also you lose treasured body heat at a quicker rate.

There are some signs of hypothermia that make it easy to recognize.

In most people, shivering is the first sign your body is too cold. That is the way the body attempts to heat itself.

If you begin having trouble talking or walking, get assistance immediately.

More information is available about hypothermia and the way to avoid it at the Wilderness Skills Institute.

Be prepared

In addition to taking along a first aid kit, consider taking a wilderness survival book with you. While you likely will not need it, these books contain information that could save your life if an emergency arises. It is easy to panic during outdoor situations. Panic is the leading cause of death in the outdoors.

On your adventures, make sure to pack lots of food and water, in case you stay longer than you intend.

There are also many small items that every hiker, camper, hunter, outdoorsman, and so forth, need to have on them at all times.

Taking the time to be prepared is the best way to keep from having an emergency when you are outdoors. If you have lots of equipment handy and feel assured in your capability to handle any situation, you will have more fun.

Live healthily

Being in top bodily condition is another way to survive while you are outside. The better shape your body is in, the much more likely you are to swim or walk lengthy distances for help if needed.

Consuming a diet rich in lean protein, whole grains, vegetables, and fruit on a regular basis is the best way to ensure health and energy.

Top 10 Tools for First Aid Kits

A first aid kit that is accessible in times of crisis should be mandatory for every house and vehicle. First aid kits can be purchased pre-assembled, or each item can be purchased individually, depending on personal preferences. Nonetheless, any first aid kit will include simple products.

First aid guide

A first aid handbook should be included with any first aid kit. This guide will help you in the treatment of fractures, sprains, bites, and other health problems. Before a disaster happens, the guide should be reviewed, so those who use the kit will know the fundamentals of first aid.

Tweezers

Tweezers are an effective resource in any first aid kit, regardless of the specific design of the kit. Tweezers can be used for extracting debris from a wound, for example, glass, gravel, or splinter. These could be used to remove bees' stingers.

Swabs in alcohol

Alcohol wipes are used before antibiotic ointment or bandages are applied in the area to clean up the contaminated or wounded region. Alcohol swabs can be used with anesthetic swabs and, if necessary, can be used to sterilize tweezers.

Antibiotic ointment

The antibiotic ointment can be used to treat many forms of infections and helps to properly heal the wound. The antibiotic ointment also helps to prevent the infection from being infected and should be given after thorough cleaning of the area.

Bandages

Multi-size adhesive bandages can form part of a first aid kit. Try buying a package of various types of bandages and adding some of them to the kit. Standard bandages are more necessary than the smallest and largest sizes, and it is also a good idea to add some additional bandages if necessary.

Pads of gauze

Adhesives are not often wide to cover a wound; therefore, it is necessary to have a first aid kit with gauze pads. Gauze pads may be used or added to a bloody bandage. Gauze pads are available in several sizes and should be supplied in each kit.

Medical tape

Surgical tape is used as it is used with bandages to protect gauze pads or wraps. This tape is designed to remove residues and is generally in a long roll.

Flexible bandages

Flexible bandages allow a sprained joint to stay motionless and decrease swelling. The

Flexible bandages are fitted with hook and loop or metal fixtures. You should tie these lightweight bandages around the feet, knees, wrists, and elbows before you see a doctor. Such bandages range between one and six inches in width.

Pain Relievers

A variety of pain relievers are needed for any first aid kit. Pain relievers such as aspirin and non-aspirin should always be included in the pack. If the house has babies, make sure that pain relievers intended for them are included. These may also be used for mild discomforts and pains when treating a deep scratch or wound.

Instant cold pack

Many medical professionals recommend that an injury be iced to avoid swelling. The cold pack is not cold until the seal is broken on the box, and the material is triggered. This form of cold pack is suitable for simple first aid kits, as it requires no freezing.

TOP 11 ITEMS

Here are the top 11 absolute must-have medical supplies for kits:

1. First Aid Manual

Gloves/eye protection

CPR mask for Pocket

Tweezers

Magnifying glass

Four r gauze pads

Surgical tape

Two triangular bandages

Splint

Flexible bandage

Medical scissors

Also, consider adding

20 mL syringe and irrigation cap

benzoic tincture

biodegradable soap

Opposite Flexi-Grip Film

Also, for remote environments and situations, all other items necessary for the management of wounds should be included starting from anesthetics , medical staples and a surgical scalpel.

Conclusion

Living in a world that's filled with surprises, sometimes pleasant and sometimes quite the opposite, we've all got to make sure that we're adequately prepared to deal with whatever is thrown at us. As a result, having a bugout bag is something that preppers and non-preppers alike should consider. In this book, we went over the things that make a good bugout bag, how to choose a bugout bag and the supplies to include. Hopefully, you've gathered a great deal of information on what you'll need in order to ensure that your 72 hour bag is as prepped as it needs to be.

www.ingramcontent.com/pod-product-compliance
Lightning Source LLC
Chambersburg PA
CBHW071844080526
44589CB00012B/1104